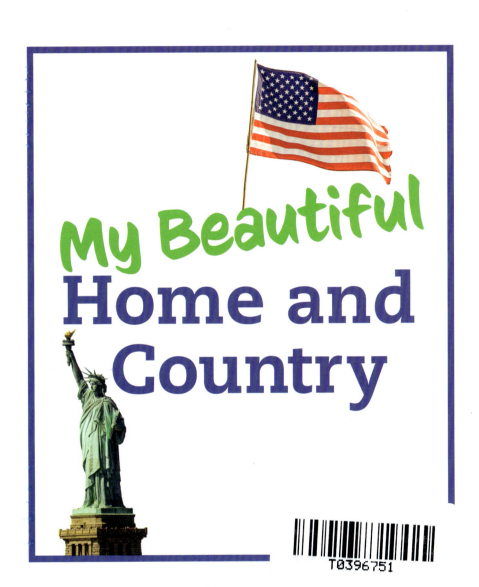

My Beautiful Home and Country

Dona Herweck Rice

United States of America

The Northeast

includes the largest U.S. city and smallest state

temperate climate

woodlands

Washington, DC

The Northeast

New York City

Atlantic Ocean

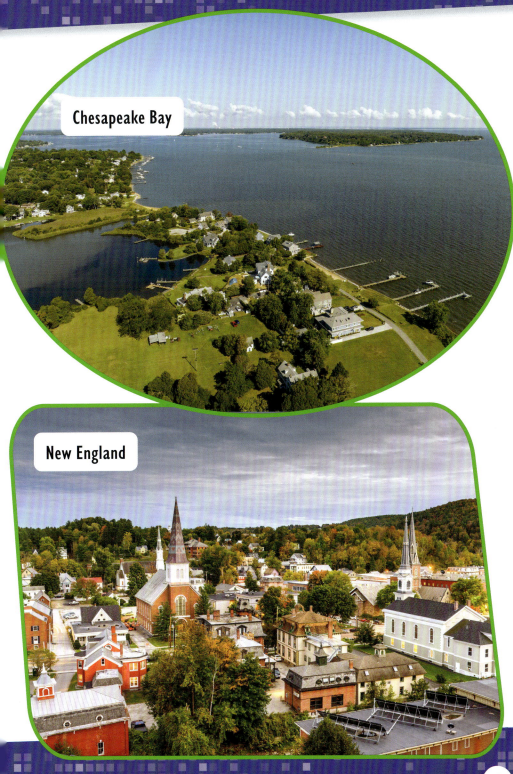

Chesapeake Bay

New England

The Southeast

includes the largest U.S. wetlands

The Southeast

bayou

hurricane

keys

Nashville, Tennessee

The Midwest

called America's heartland

Great Lakes

Chicago, Illinois

seasonal climate

The Midwest

tornado

prairie

Badlands

agriculture

The Rocky Mountain States

includes the largest U.S. mountain range

The Rocky Mountain States

Glacier National Park

Denver, Colorado

Yellowstone National Park

Bryce Canyon National Park

The Southwest

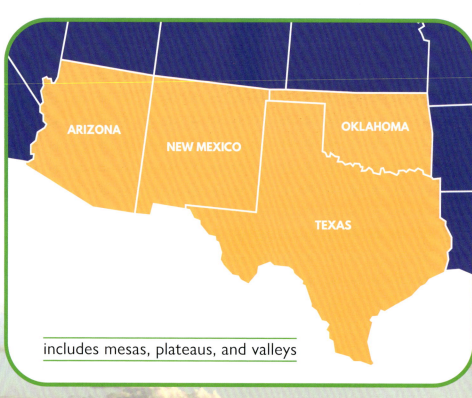

ARIZONA · NEW MEXICO · OKLAHOMA · TEXAS

includes mesas, plateaus, and valleys

arid climate

Grand Canyon National Park

pueblos

The Southwest

oil field

San Antonio River

rodeo

Gulf of Mexico

The West

has rain forests, deserts, and a long coastline

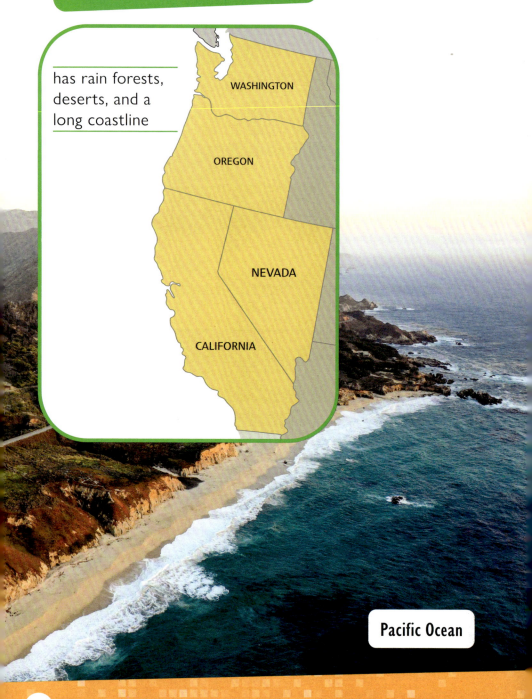

WASHINGTON
OREGON
NEVADA
CALIFORNIA

Pacific Ocean

rainy-to-arid climate

redwoods

25

The West

desert

beach

tourism

Las Vegas, Nevada

Alaska

largest state

Arctic climate

Hawai'i

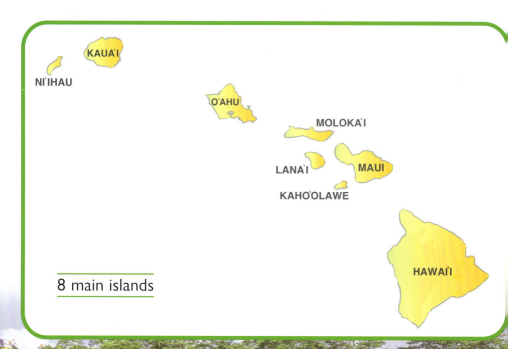

8 main islands

tropical climate

Consultant
Cheryl Lane, M.Ed.
Secondary Teacher

Publishing Credits
Rachelle Cracchiolo, M.S.Ed., Publisher
Emily R. Smith, M.A.Ed., *SVP of Content Development*
Véronique Bos, *VP of Creative*
Fabiola Sepulveda, *Art Director*

Image Credits: all images from iStock, Shutterstock, or in the public domain

Library of Congress Control Number available upon request.

This book may not be reproduced or distributed in any way without prior written consent from the publisher.

5482 Argosy Avenue
Huntington Beach, CA 92649
www.tcmpub.com
ISBN 979-8-3309-0486-0
© 2025 Teacher Created Materials, Inc.
Printed by: 51497
Printed in: China